Resonant Ruminations

Unni

India | USA | UK

Copyright © Unni
All Rights Reserved.

This book has been self-published with all reasonable efforts taken to make the material error-free by the author. No part of this book shall be used, reproduced in any manner whatsoever without written permission from the author, except in the case of brief quotations embodied in critical articles and reviews.

The Author of this book is solely responsible and liable for its content including but not limited to the views, representations, descriptions, statements, information, opinions, and references ["Content"]. The Content of this book shall not constitute or be construed or deemed to reflect the opinion or expression of the Publisher or Editor. Neither the Publisher nor Editor endorse or approve the Content of this book or guarantee the reliability, accuracy, or completeness of the Content published herein and do not make any representations or warranties of any kind, express or implied, including but not limited to the implied warranties of merchantability, fitness for a particular purpose.

The Publisher and Editor shall not be liable whatsoever...

Made with ❤ on the BookLeaf Publishing Platform
www.bookleafpub.in
www.bookleafpub.com

Dedication

My book hopefully contributes to the necessary virtue in this world; spiraling into greedy mania and deprivation of humanity with demotivated minds that are falling behind the hinders failing to envision their purpose of being a better person.

Preface

The world has changed... Amidst the surroundings one gets nowhere trying to learn what's going on around him. Sometimes The world proves itself to be a realm of void where violence spreads across like a cattle herd on grazing land, a brawl or dispute over misconceptions where in it hooks on the events based on love, relations, interactions and so on. Loss of humanity has been severe since one fails to observe his purpose as the Earth's bloodline who ought to be honest, modest, kind and humane. Moreover, the forgetfulness in a man's life about a hereafter which severely makes him prone to be inhumane.

Acknowledgements

With warm and sincere thanks to the God, the Almighty that helped and stood by me from the very starting to the end where my pen stopped swirling further more. Also, thanks to my beloved teacher Mrs. Shani for her relentless support, hard work and enthusiasm to see me becoming a published poet; my parents who shared their wishes and support; my grandparents who would support me no matter what my interest is; my elder brother who told me to keep going; my other teachers who always supported me in my good interests; my cousins who praised me for my good work; my friends Ihsan, Nibraz, Amal, Adnan, Ridha and Sana who stood by my good interests and works no matter what.

1. The Last Call

In the uncautioned mind of a body,
where he glides along, finding attractiveness in his life
of
bliss and joy.
He was strong and firm with a mind of
arrogance, healthy with deep pockets where
life for him,
was a soft little piece of cake.

Oh! Little did he knew,
all his might and health
along with his opulence
would do nothing for him,
all in just a snap of a finger.

The owner of arrogance
who forgot of himself before the supreme provider,
was the holder of the biggest blunder too.

"A mind immersed in conceit.

A pride unable to be measured".

Rowed and rowed along the honey stream,
Just the last few to be rowed.
The moment changed as a hanging bat,
when he got off and stood at the end.

"The honey stream turned chili sauce".

The time has come and started ringing
the final call.
Confused and trembled the arrogant,
Jumped off, ran and tried hiding.

Worsened!

The final one-time visitor left it all behind,
except the arrogant.

2. The Wilted Remains of the Treasure

In the whispers of the wind
I hear your name.
And in the silence of the wind
I still hear your name...
My voice inside.

I see your face glimpsing in the gloomy rooms
as glimpsing you from the gathered crowds
of strange moving faces.

Oh lord! what was that
violation I broke,
Oh Master! what was that
blunder I undertook.

All the fun we had,
the moments we shared
and the games we played,
made us to fill our chambers with...

Tight and hard.

Someday I hope this mist
Keeping us apart fades away,
I'm sure we'll then meet
right away.

3. The Nature of Sun and Moon

He wakes up from his
lovely cozy slumber,
off he goes jumping off of his
crib to the world outside.

The naughty bright sun
pursued to shine to his very full,
outwitting and fooling off the dear mother moon.

He was in him,
as strong as a beast,
as brave as a lion and as bright and sharp as a raven.

But as always and usual,
the little bright sun turned white and blue and hid rear of
the dear mother moon
after seeing them strange visitor stars.

4. The Loop of Greed

He has got all the power
he wants in his piece.
He looks for the rest and
seizes them to place his throne.

He fights the wimps for their
pieces with the power he has got.
Outflows the great river from
the dismayed eyes of the oppressed
pieces.

He who has forgotten his weight in
his piece in the depth of greed...

He has got all the bread
he craves.
He had in him, the spark of envy ignited to a flame of
greed
after glimpsing pockets deeper than his.

He who disliked his blessings
in the strangle of his greed...

They who were taught to keep
affection above all,
had wobbling minds only to be
gobbled up by the maws of
greed.

The tireless lust for power and
opulence conceives the vivid
testimony of greed, thus never cracking
the loop of greed.

5. A Tale of Two Natures

There came by an alpinist,
deep down from the
valley of misty cover,
Now who wants a warm safe shelter.

A nice black cave that
caught his eyes
made his mind
precarious enough to fall for it as shelter.

Entered the trekker into
the cavern, his veins strangling
his shivering heart...

He stood stiff before
the two trails inside;
dark and still
that had his glance.

Off he went in to one

with the final sips from his flagon
of courage...

Stunned by his sight
of a dwell ablaze
by the scarlet blaze,
All right before him.

Walked out curiously and
headed for the next;
returned the alpinist
a sense of relief.

He came up before a musty dwell
where he lit up the room with
a set of fine fire log on the side;
startled to witness the ruby flame,
Once again...

Off he went to put off
his gear and get his
fine comfy blazer and
reappeared at the coincident.

Startled by his sight as
the blaze was already doused.
But in the first space as he went,

The ruby blaze remained unfazed.

6. A Loyal Soul

The tree that stood tall,
has a canvas that is
enduring the rhythmic
drumming of the yaffle.

The tree that stood tall,
has a bark that suffers
the diabolical sheer of
an arm.

The ached prey still
offers its fare, the
peaceful sighs of cool
breeze and a touch
of charm with its
crispy veil, all to
the menaces

7. A Warrior's Life

A mighty gladiator walking
through the isolated path
of a mountain wearing
robes of snow.

Only from a stone's throw,
he perceives in a trice;
a huge maniacal wild beast
charging from the rear.

Out came his arm
slicing the frosty breeze.
Discharged from him
a splendid sheer of his sword.

Dodged by the threat
now leapt onto him
digging its fangs on him
and left the prey mauled...

He wakes up in pain
and sets off crawling.
His movements; sluggish
and torturous like a
fumbling alpinist.

The potent warrior discerned
his blunder in a fortnight
when nature and time pampered
him to cure his wound...

Periods crossed by as once
again, the warrior clashed
with the same foe; but an
army of them that were
Slain by the single force.

8. The Rust and the Reverence

The horse that is now
startled with all ears by
the forced summoning of
his soul by his keeper;
The knight.

The keeper's effort was
for that reason, his
pet would be delighted
firstly, but hates a while after.

He was fed an average
entrée and some
drizzle and trickle
to wash them down...

Off they went promptly
to the ground of martyrs.
A piece that had fallen

off from the hell and
descended gently to the
earth where the innocent
souls are traded for pride.

He gallops fast where his
hooves are molten red
that emits blazing sparks
from the rusty scrubs
on the molten grounds.

The eyes of the horse
glancing through the
narrow space granted
by its eye lids due
to the boiling heatwaves.

His trembling eyes roams
around where he feels
the violence, scream,
slashes of arms and
the heat of blood.

The poor creature yearns
to go back to its peaceful
home, but how could he?
He's got to be grateful to

his keeper for his meal.

9. On Gazing at Your Forgotten Deeds

A vigorous mortal in
a good old hamlet was
a mighty sinner but
with the miracle of
Perceivance and time,
the evil actor had
received a noble change
in himself.

He was indeed a prostitute
himself; a maniacal sensualist.
He was indeed a pickpocket
himself; quite a burglar.

He found melodious music
from the weeping of his
victims he tortured.

He felt the triumph in

his veins from the
sobbing of his victims
he snatched.

On a fine cloudy evening
where he was running
Through the woods far
away from his land.

His arms carried some
glittering jewels from
his prey today.

Only from a stone's throw,
he glanced upon a pond
Of sparkling crystals.
The sinner went up to
it for a glance of his
noble victorious face...

The pride and triumph on his
face faded in a trice when he saw
what he perceived.

The sinner was staring
and hearing his sins
in the reflection of the

pond's still waters.

He was struck by
a bolt of lightning piercing
Through the thin air...

With a noble change
in his core and veins,
he tossed the elegance
Into the reflecting pond.

And that has made all the
miracles...

10. Just Try it!

Franklin! just hear me
Out!
Please eat this apple
so,
You would stop getting
sick all the
Time.
It tastes good, trust me,
just try it!

(Fine! But I am sick of
this nagging!
I wish I am not told what
to do all the time) ...

A big bright smile
stretched on Franklin's
face as he
tried it.

Franklin! just hear me
out!
Don't play with that
knife!...
Fine, you can do it at
your own risk.
I won't tell you
twice!

(Finally! at least once
I'm not being told
what to do) ...

Franklin's face turned
bitterly dull as a
cut landed on his
Pinky.

Dear daddy was profoundly
hurt too, but concealed
his joy underneath of
letting him inherit the miracles of
the unknown by allowing him
to just try it.

11. Ignition of Willingness

Robert the sufferer,
who was enduring
the torture of his
empty pockets which
burdened him gently
during his days of
lavish debt.

His home was for him;
As lonely and haunted
as if besieged by a
horde of phantoms
in the darkest midnight
where the moon
yearned for light.

One way and nothing
more to break free
from the menaces;
was to plunge into the

trench at his very
next step; its mouth
hindering the horde
with sacred light beams.

The trench was indeed
gravely dark and haunting.
An obligating instant to
ignite his willingness...

With the very last
drops of his spirit,
he leant ahead and
dived into it like
Jerry made his way
into Tom's maws...

Robert woke up with
an amazing glow of sight.
His home felt neither
besieged nor haunting;
But still puzzling.

The victim only learned
shortly after, that his
audacity to dive has
Bought all the changes.

12. On the Other Side

The thing I learned
in the hell I lived,
was on the other side,
lied a heaven to glide.

13. Demolition of Sympathy

A freshly moulded one
from the essentials of
Saplings to sky touching
trunks land its feet
down on the home.

It shines with the
rays of innocence,
while bearing the
divinely heart of God.

Once grown enough,
the rays can be
hindered from and
fades the brilliant heart;
being caught by the intrusion
of avarice;
That's what they say.

But if you ask me,

the hindrance of brilliance
And the intruding
darkness requires envy too.

14. The Spiral of Liability

The harshly wounded man
who've been mauled by,
the inevitable vicious bear
that trespassed his home
is now laying at a corner
in his room after ousting
The threat from his county.

He who was shedding
his tears in the already
flooded room with the
downpour of agony,
is now giggling with the
barrel of agony in his
heart reminiscing his
concluded past.

He was indeed, once
a boy; who could
hook it from the

burden caused by the
trespassing sheep.

15. From Where Not to Look Back; The Stairs of Reflection

Heidi, the little dreamer
who, yearned for a slumber
in the sky castle far
and high above this maniacal sphere.

The dreamer wished, the
resident angels of the
Sky castle to read her
bedtime tales prior the slumber.

Little Heidi did take all
the nights not for granted;
as the little steadfast dreamed
for her wish to be fulfilled
as she sits on the facade
of the house, where she gazed
at the hazy skies after nightfall.

"In the back of several cycles
of the revolving orbs,
the hoper's awaited wishes
aroused to be fulfilled during one of those nights".

Overwhelmed at the discerned
sight where in a stone's throw,
stood tall an ascended
escalier before the little frow.

Blasted off towards it the
dreamer, as she perceived the
cloudpiercing standing escalator,
calmly waited for her.

Little Heidi vigorously climbed up
the stairs only to step up
and look back beneath her
after Knowing she's reached its core.

The dreamer was terrorized
by the sight and wanted
back, but soon felt deceived.
"And she never looked back; she ascended."

16. He's Got the Best Plans!

The piece of paper I found
in my backyard had the
footsteps to the cave inflated
with life cuddling pride
of fortune; hidden in the
infamous vault...

I packed my inevitables
for the journey as
the sun still dozing;
hoping to pass the woods
for my purpose.

My intimate who knew it
along me conceived
the threat paved
through the lurking woods;
stepped into my track
persuading me to change roads...

At the core of that night,
my booned friend sacrificed
his named woolly be mauled
by the maws of woods;
liberated it from the
village's noble seizure.

The loss of the ewe into
the wild flickered the
gleam of perceivance of its
death into the village's
conscious that struck.

The steadfast one, to myself;
the scent of the carcass
breezed past; I decided
To switch roads.

17. Slumber of Devotion

That moment in a soul's core,
where one lives in the trickling
honey drops of his hourglass;
oblivious about the haunting
bitterness of life.

That moment, when God
himself flicked off the
skies for my love to be
cuddled in the warmth
of my wings dozing
on the couch of adoration.

I was aroused by the
love scented breeze that
trespassed through the
windows refusing to be closed.

My wings pulled her closer
as it flew through her veiled hair

while the night sang its musical silence.

18. The Hesitation of Luck

Captain Rhuba'arb, the holder
of 'The Gold Pirates' was a
mighty reigner of the sea;
'The Honored One', who
moulded himself from bruises
that scarred.

Silver Hawk, 'The Lucky
Charm' was the ally
of the crown and
the leader of 'The Hawk Pirates'...

The allies, who held
'The Death' by his
scythe is now held
by him to be drowned.

They who came across
a sea swirling kraken,
pulled out their cutlass

from its clothes with a
hiss of nightmare...

The tentacled creature,
who posed a harm
on their sky splitting
voyage as a dual;
promoted itself to the summit
of stupidity.

The grisly monster realised
its place as it drowned
deep down, being slashed
away by the crowned
butcher even when, 'The
Lucky Charm' stumbled to glow.

19. Disarming the Disputes

The way I shut down
my crave to rectify
that soul's delusion,
who is now my
heart's cohesion in
the most weary
times of journey
and a companion in
the strive for my vision;
now discerns my
soul the best I had done.

20. Gazing from a Ledge at the Midnight

Oh, you the silver queen
of the infallible stars
of the dark painted world.
Your smile lit up the world
like a head steamed king finally smiled.

In a night so dark
that fades their eyes,
I acquire your gaze
from this ledge so far.

You indeed are
miraculously meaningful.
If I was good to you;
You will be back as an angel.
But if I did thee bad;
You sure be returning as him Lucifer.
I always knew that.
I always knew that.

21. Scattered Fragments of God's Love

The world she sees high
above from the blue sky
must be mesmerizing;
one's dream be there forever gliding.

She can be there forever
if her soul wishes to
indulge in the hypnotising beauty
leaving behind what she's obliged to.

She can keep herself,
the worldly riches and offerings;
if her soul wishes to.
But she was conferred by
the God; a piece of love and kindness
of himself.

She's devoted to return
to her chirping chicks;

bestowing upon them
the worldly riches and offerings.

www.ingramcontent.com/pod-product-compliance
Lightning Source LLC
Chambersburg PA
CBHW070039070426
42449CB00012BA/3102